# MEL BAY'S

MW00580802

# TAB ONLY METHOD
## WILLIAM BAY

## ONLINE AUDIO

## To Access the Online Audio Go to:
## www.melbay.com/22141BCDEB

# How to Hold the Guitar & Pick

The correct way to hold the guitar

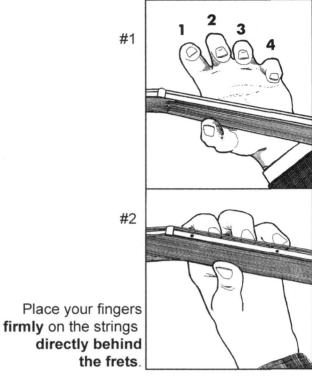

**#1**

**#2**

Place your fingers **firmly** on the strings **directly behind the frets**.

**◼ = Down Stroke of the Pick.**

**#1**

This is the pick

**#2**

Hold it in this manner firmly between the thumb and first finger.

**#3**

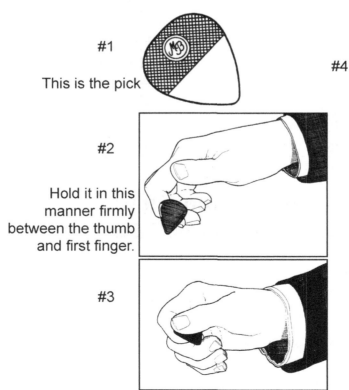

**#4**

# Tuning the Guitar

The six open strings of the guitar will be of the same pitch as the six notes shown in the illustration

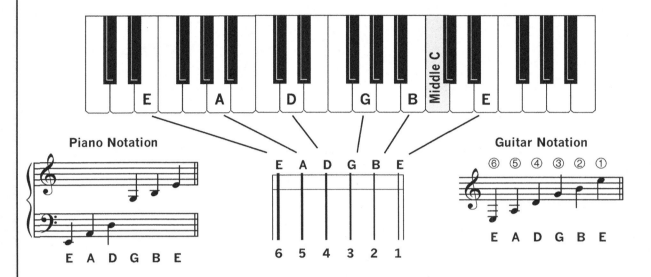

Piano Notation

Guitar Notation

E A D G B E

6 5 4 3 2 1

E A D G B E

## Another Method of Tuning

1. Tune the 6th string unison with the **E** or 12th white key to the **left** of **middle C** on the piano.

2. Place the finger behind the fifth fret of the 6th string. This will give you the tone or pitch of the 5th string (**A**).

3. Place finger behind the fifth fret of the 5th string to get the pitch of the 4th string (**D**).

4. Repeat same procedure to obtain the pitch of the 3rd string (**G**).

5. Place finger behind the fourth fret of the 3rd string to get the pitch of the 2nd string (**B**).

6. Place finger behind the fifth fret of the 2nd string to get the pitch of the 1st string (**E**).

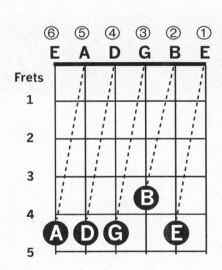

# Electronic Guitar Tuner

Electronic Guitar Tuners are available at your music store. They are a handy device and highly recommended.

# Notes

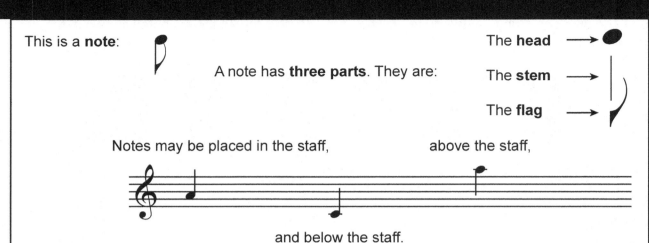

This is a **note**:

A note has **three parts**. They are:

The **head** →

The **stem** →

The **flag** →

Notes may be placed in the staff,      above the staff,

and below the staff.

A note will bear the name of the line or space it occupies on the staff.
The location of a note in, above, or below the staff will indicate the pitch.

**Pitch:** the height or depth of a tone.
**Tone:** a musical sound.

# Types of Notes

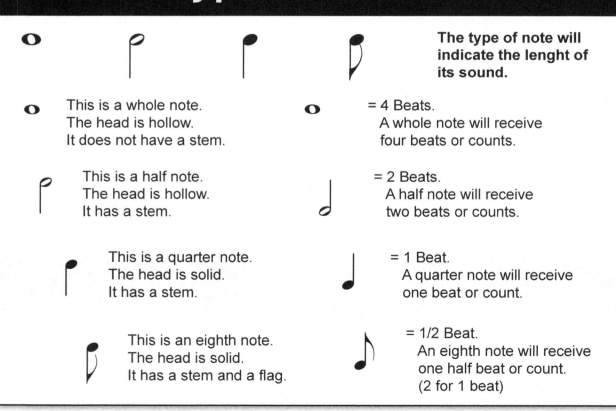

**The type of note will indicate the lenght of its sound.**

This is a whole note.
The head is hollow.
It does not have a stem.

= 4 Beats.
A whole note will receive four beats or counts.

This is a half note.
The head is hollow.
It has a stem.

= 2 Beats.
A half note will receive two beats or counts.

This is a quarter note.
The head is solid.
It has a stem.

= 1 Beat.
A quarter note will receive one beat or count.

This is an eighth note.
The head is solid.
It has a stem and a flag.

= 1/2 Beat.
An eighth note will receive one half beat or count.
(2 for 1 beat)

# Rest

A **rest** is a sign used to designate a period of silence.

This is an eighth rest.　　　　　　　This is a quarter rest.

Half rest.　　　　　　　　　　　Whole rest.
Half rest lie on the line　　　　　Whole rest hang down
　　　　　　　　　　　　　　　　from the line.

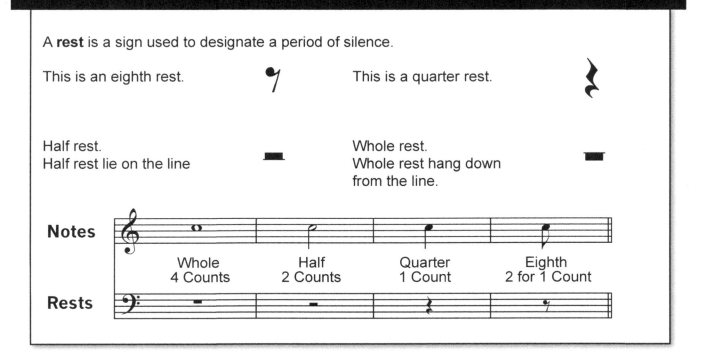

| | Whole<br>4 Counts | Half<br>2 Counts | Quarter<br>1 Count | Eighth<br>2 for 1 Count |

**Notes**

**Rests**

# The Time Signature

The above examples are the common types of time signatures to be used in this book.

The number of beats per measure. ⟶ **4** ⟵ Beats per measure.

The type of note receiving one beat. ⟶ **4** ⟵ A quarter note receives one beat.

 Signifies so-called **common time** and is simply another way of designating 4/4 time.

# Learning to Read Tablature

Tablature is a way of writing guitar music which tells you where to find notes. In tablature:

> **Lines = Strings**
> **Numbers = Frets**

## Lines = Strings

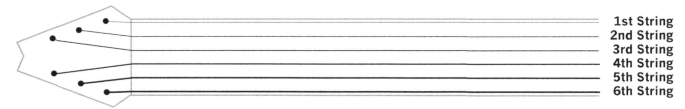

## Numbers = Frets

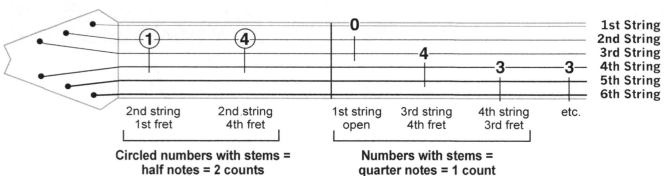

## Time values in TAB

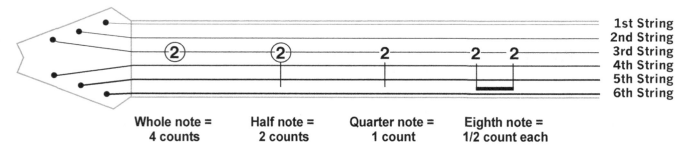

# Notes on the E String

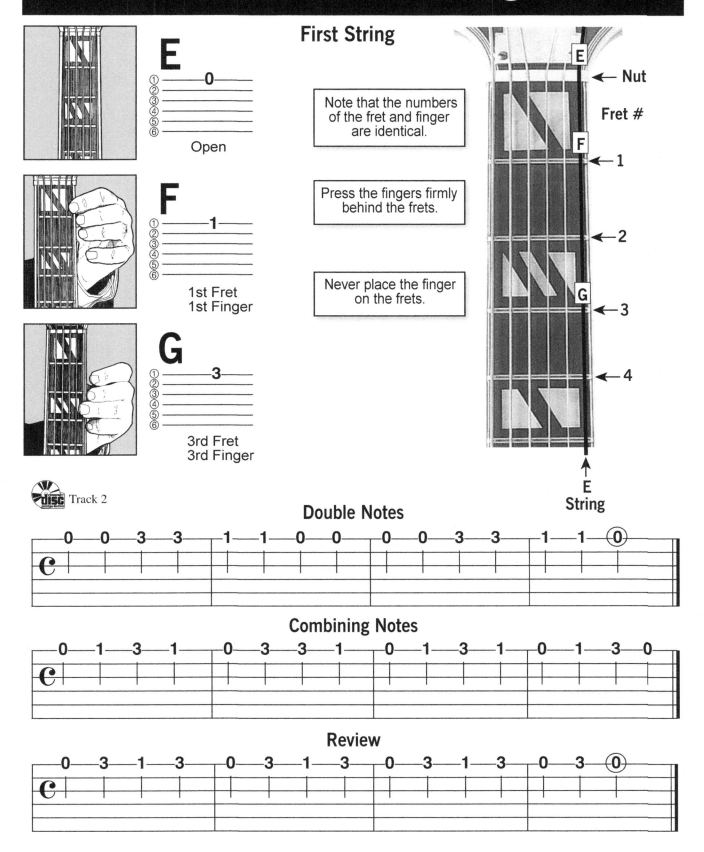

### First String

E
① ——— 0 ———
②
③
④
⑤
⑥
Open

F
① ——— 1 ———
②
③
④
⑤
⑥
1st Fret
1st Finger

G
① ——— 3 ———
②
③
④
⑤
⑥
3rd Fret
3rd Finger

Note that the numbers of the fret and finger are identical.

Press the fingers firmly behind the frets.

Never place the finger on the frets.

← Nut

Fret #

E
F
← 1
← 2
G
← 3
← 4
E
String

Track 2

### Double Notes

0  0  3  3 | 1  1  0  0 | 0  0  3  3 | 1  1  ⓪

### Combining Notes

0  1  3  1 | 0  3  3  1 | 0  1  3  1 | 0  1  3  0

### Review

0  3  1  3 | 0  3  1  3 | 0  3  1  3 | 0  3  ⓪

# Notes on the B String

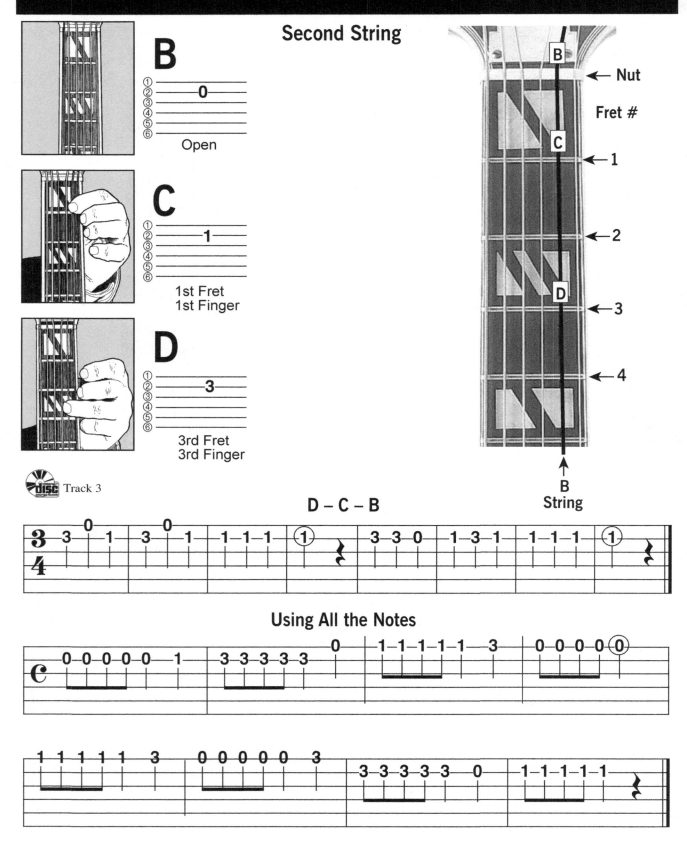

**Second String**

**B**
Open

**C**
1st Fret
1st Finger

**D**
3rd Fret
3rd Finger

Track 3

**D – C – B**

**Using All the Notes**

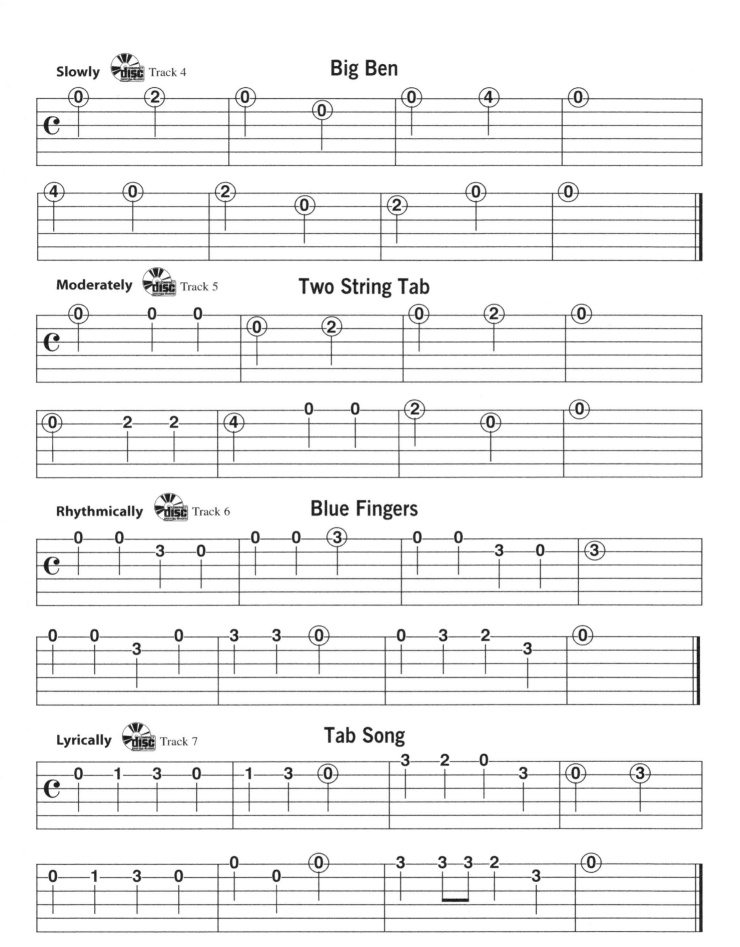

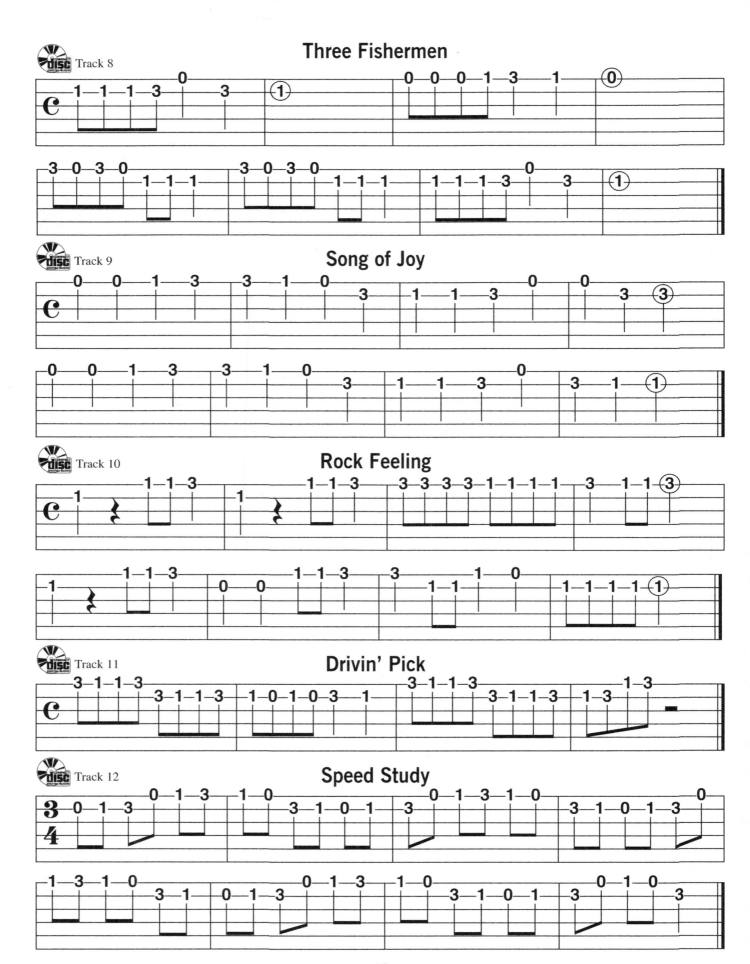

# Tab Solos
### (using 1st String and Open 6th String)

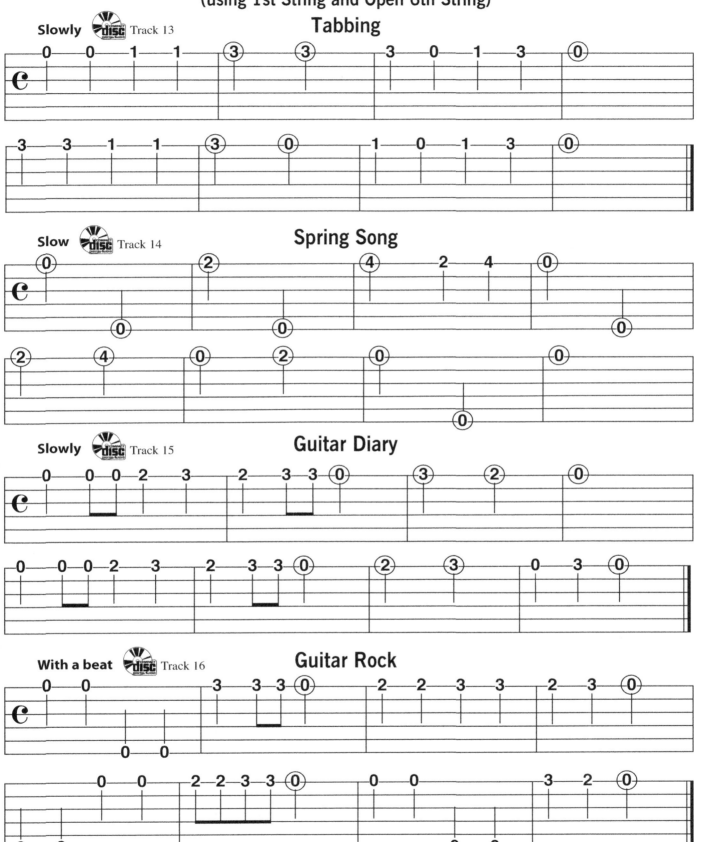

# The Tie

A **tie** is a curved line that connects two notes of the same pitch. With a tie you pick **only** the first note.

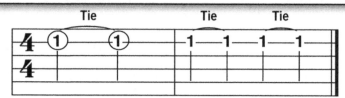

## Tie Study

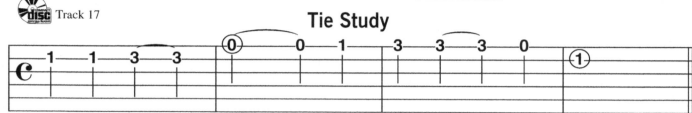

# Dotted Half Note

A **dotted half note** receives 3 beats.

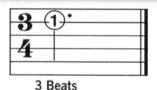

3 Beats

## Dotted Half Note Study

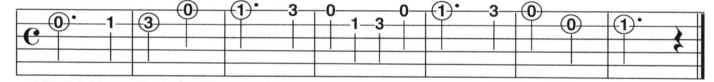

# The Slur/Hammer-on/Pull-off

A **slur** is a curved line that connects two or more notes of a different pitch. When a slur occurs, pick **only** the first note. The remaining notes are fingered but not picked. A slur going up in pitch is sometimes called a **hammer-on**. A slur going down in pitch is sometimes called a **pull-off**.

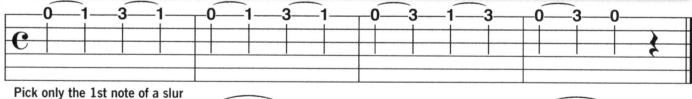

**Pick only the 1st note of a slur**

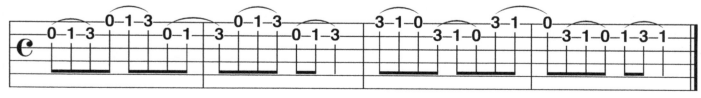

# Notes on the G String

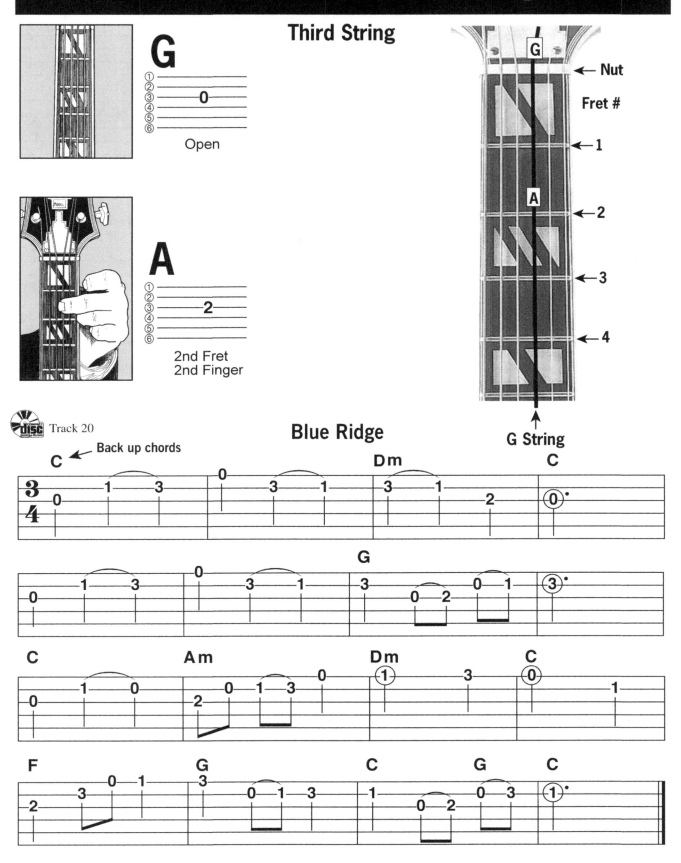

G

①
②
③ —0—
④
⑤
⑥

Open

A

①
②
③
④ —2—
⑤
⑥

2nd Fret
2nd Finger

Third String

G ← Nut

Fret #

← 1

A ← 2

← 3

← 4

G String

Track 20

## Blue Ridge

# Review of the First 3 Strings
## Running the Strings

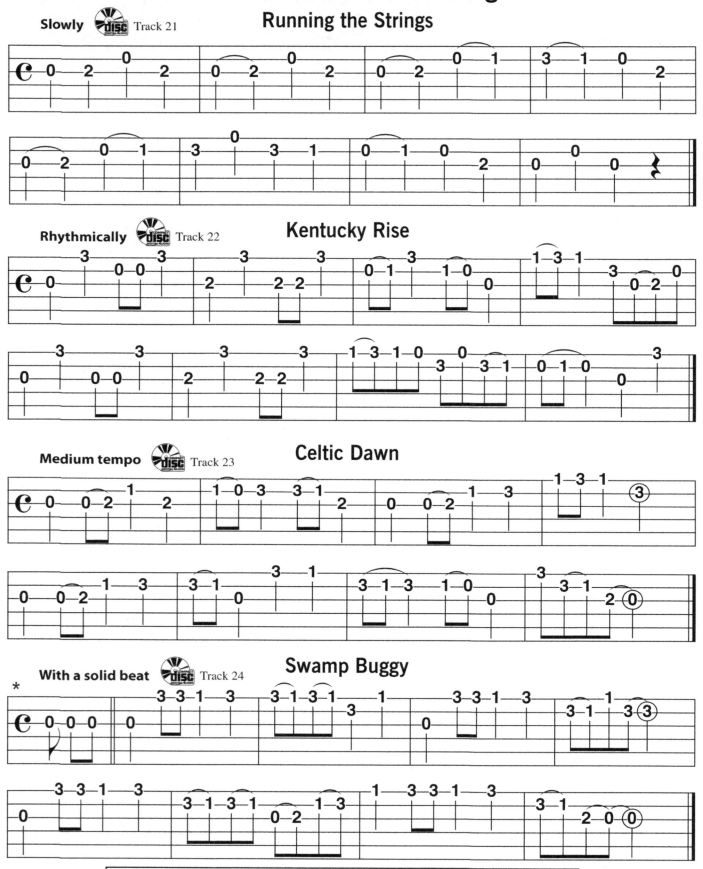

**Slowly** Track 21

**Rhythmically** Track 22 — **Kentucky Rise**

**Medium tempo** Track 23 — **Celtic Dawn**

**With a solid beat** Track 24 — **Swamp Buggy**

* Pick-up notes are notes leading into the downbeat of the first measure of a song.

14

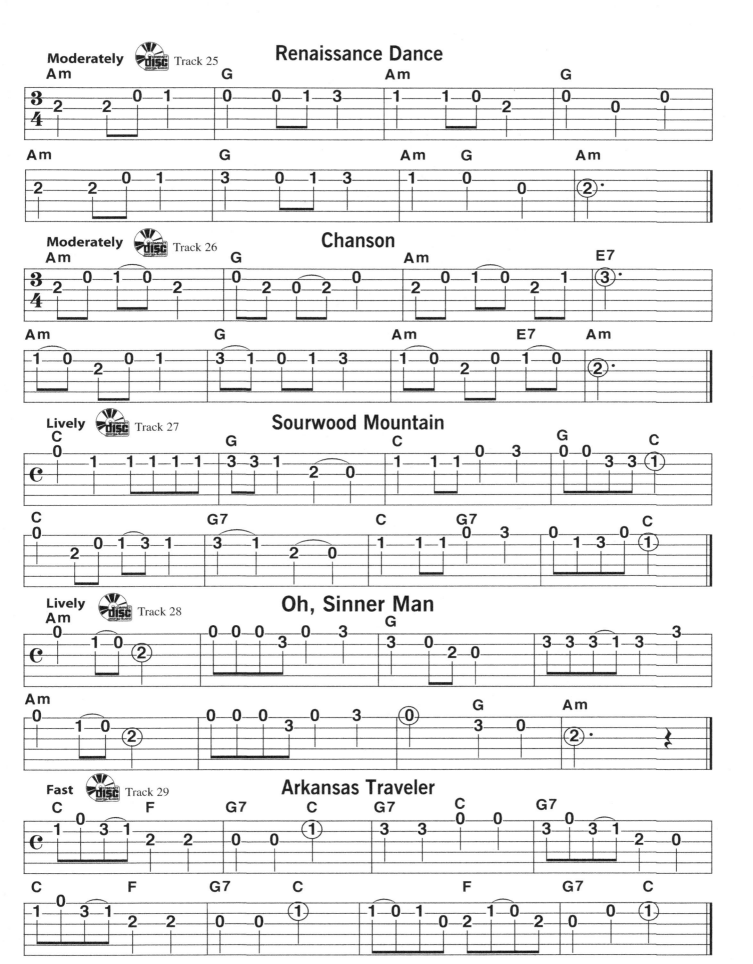

# The Slide

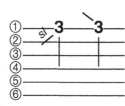

A **slide** is indicated with a *slanted line* and/or an *"sl"* written before a note. If the line slants up to the note, slide from two frets below to the written note. If the line slants down to the note, slide from two frets above to the written note. If two notes are connected with a slanted line, pick the first note and without picking the string again, slide the same finger on the string to the second note.

# Tab Solos on the First 3 Strings

Remember: The lines show what string you play. The numbers show you what fret to play.

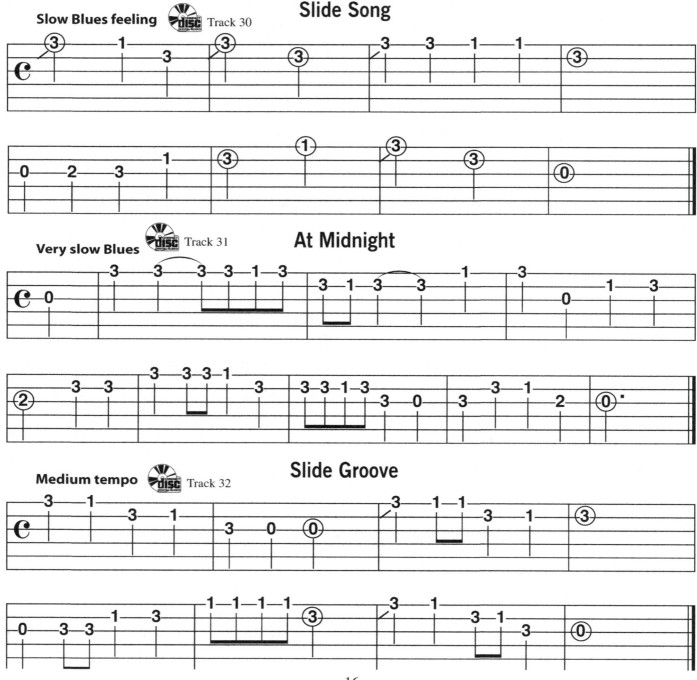

16

# Playing Several Notes at Once

When numbers appear right above one another, more than one note is played at the same time.

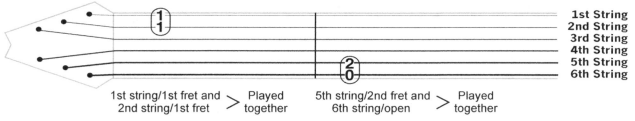

1st string/1st fret and 2nd string/1st fret > Played together

5th string/2nd fret and 6th string/open > Played together

**Circled numbers without stems = whole notes = 4 counts**

## Double Stops/Triads

When two or more notes are written on top of each other, play the notes at the same time.
Figure out the placement of the notes, beginning with the top note.

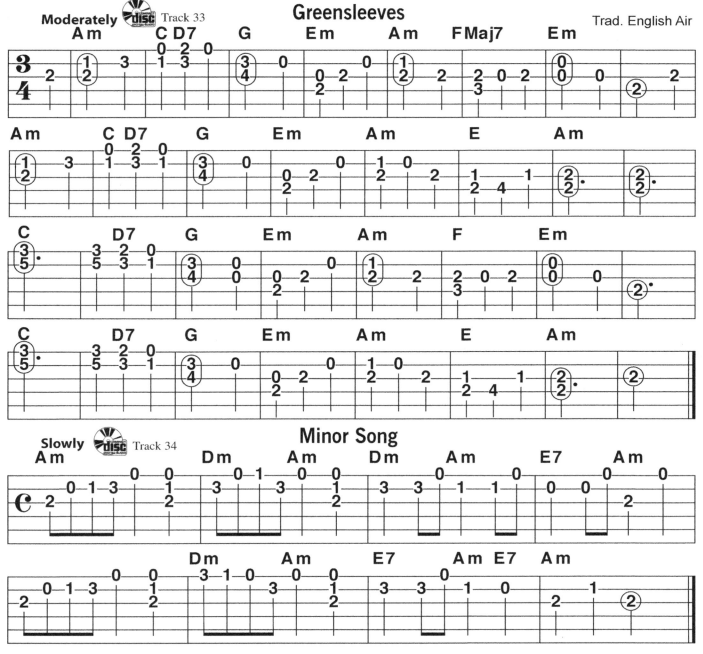

**Greensleeves**

Moderately Track 33

Trad. English Air

**Minor Song**

Slowly Track 34

17

# Notes on the D String

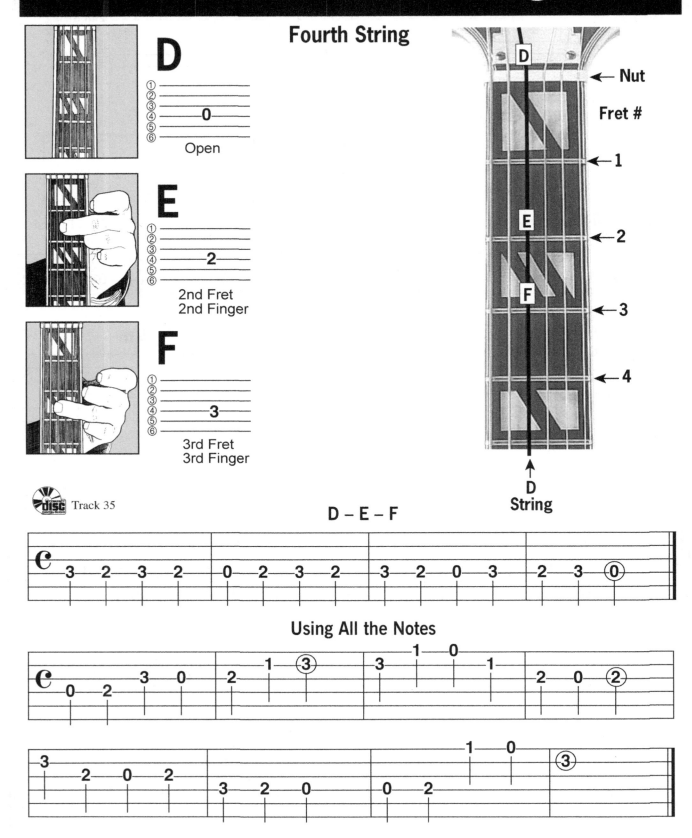

**Fourth String**

**D**

① ——————
② ——————
③ ——————
④ ————0————
⑤ ——————
⑥ ——————

Open

**E**

① ——————
② ——————
③ ——————
④ ————2————
⑤ ——————
⑥ ——————

2nd Fret
2nd Finger

**F**

① ——————
② ——————
③ ——————
④ ————3————
⑤ ——————
⑥ ——————

3rd Fret
3rd Finger

Track 35

**D – E – F**

**Using All the Notes**

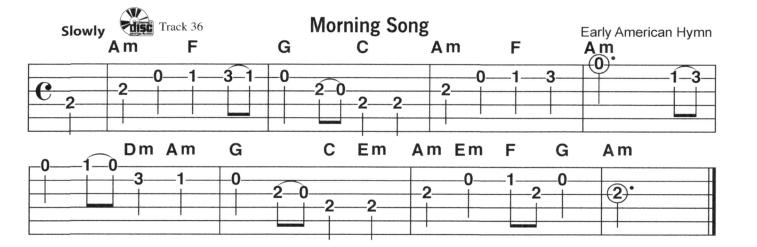

## Repeat Sign

Repeat signs look like this:

When they occur, repeat the music found between the signs

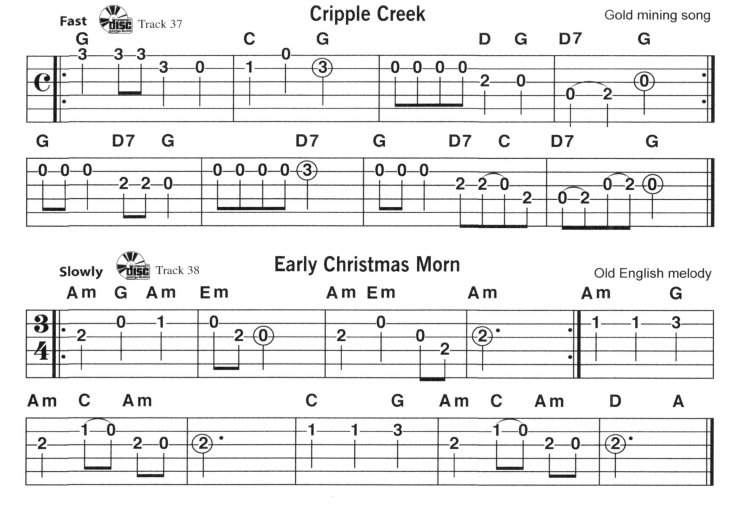

19

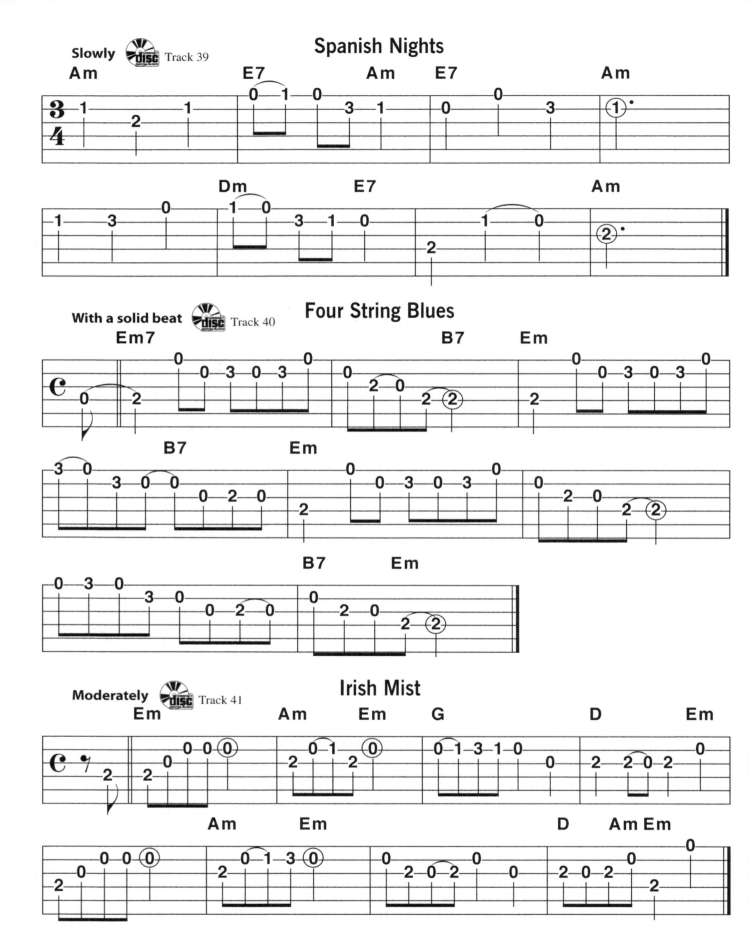

# 4 String Tab

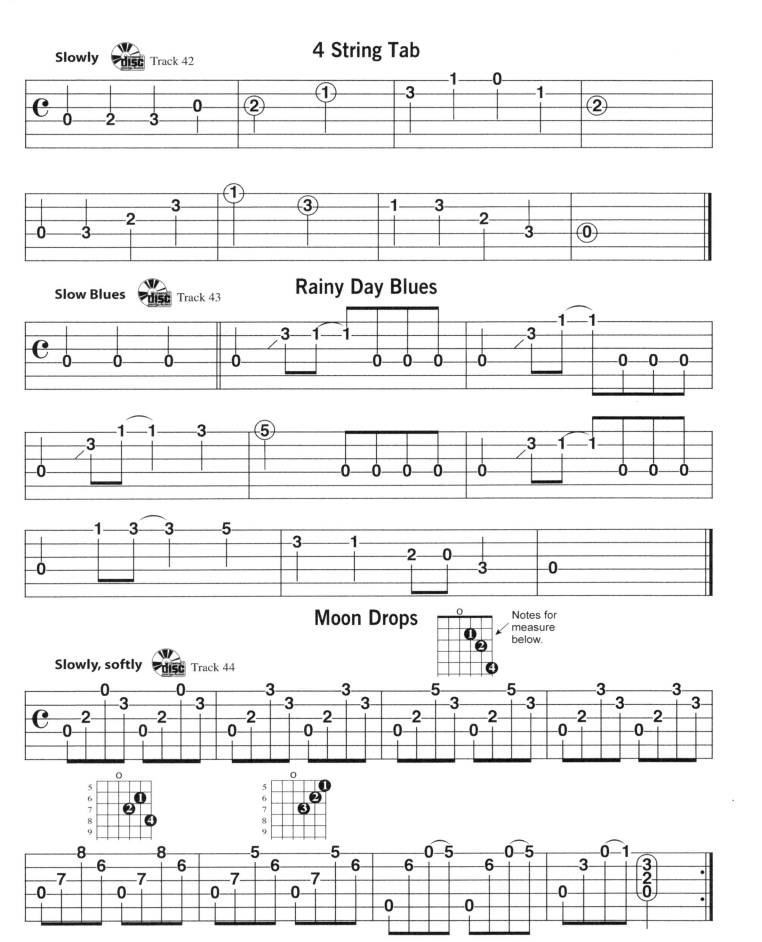

# Notes on the A String

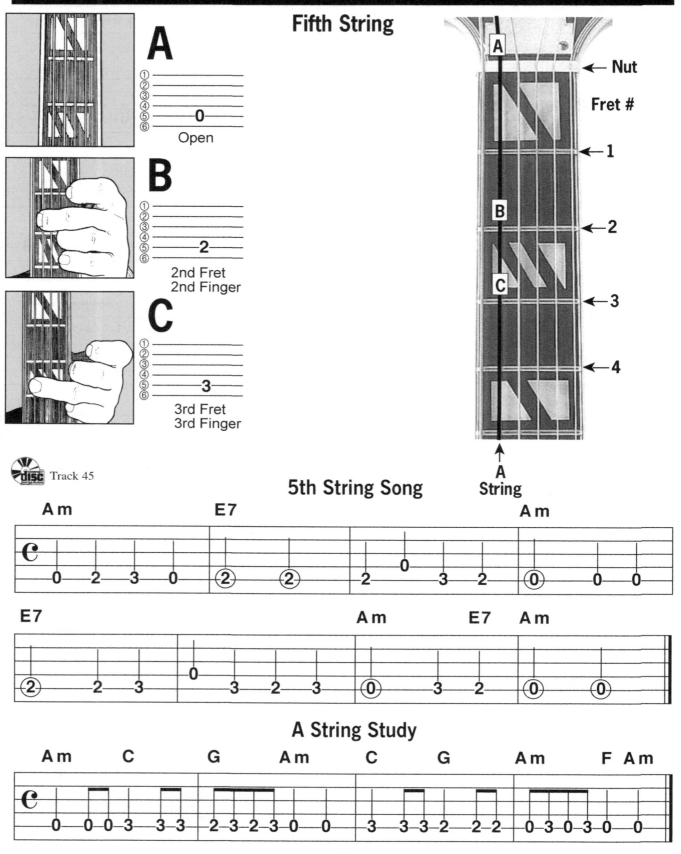

**Fifth String**

A — Open

B — 2nd Fret, 2nd Finger

C — 3rd Fret, 3rd Finger

Nut

Fret #

Track 45

## 5th String Song

## A String Study

# First and Second Ending

Sometimes in a song a first and second ending appear. When this occurs, take the first ending and observe the repeat sign. Then, on the second time through, skip the first ending, play the second ending, and continue on with the music. (Sometimes the song will end with the second ending.)

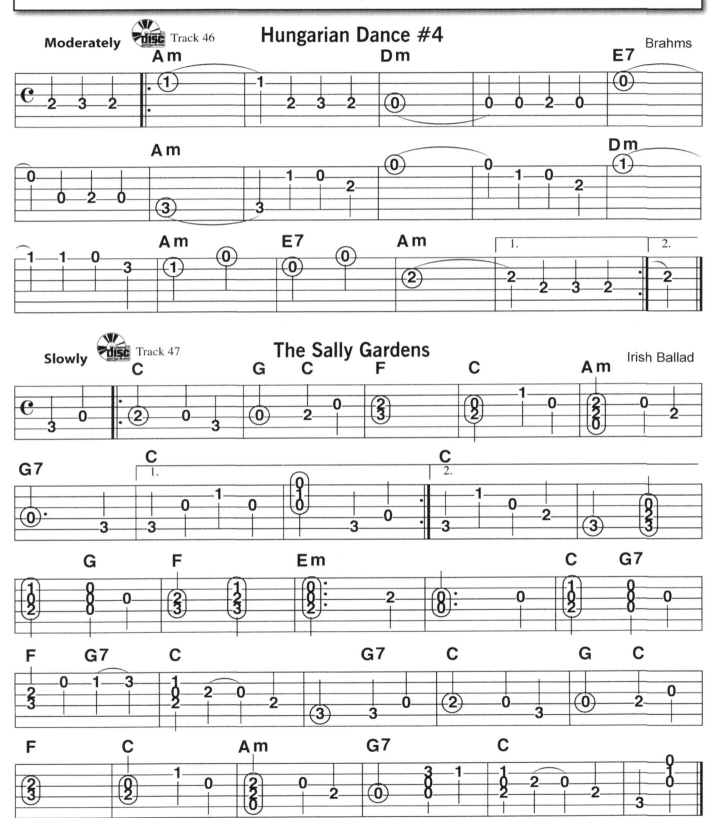

# Tab Solos

## Sao Paolo

**Flowing**

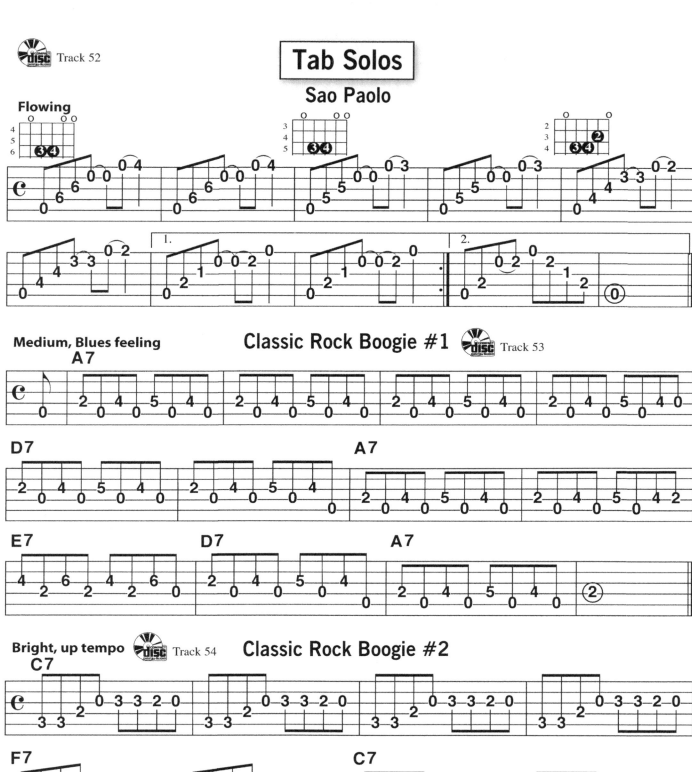

**Medium, Blues feeling**

## Classic Rock Boogie #1

Track 53

**Bright, up tempo** Track 54

## Classic Rock Boogie #2

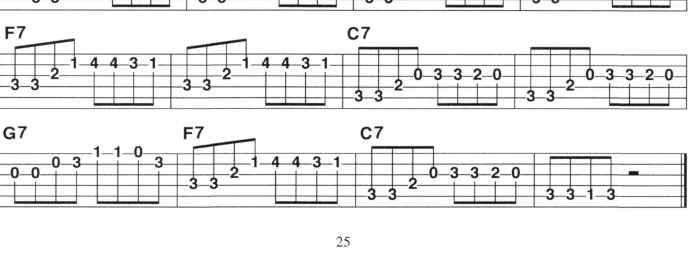

# Notes on the E String

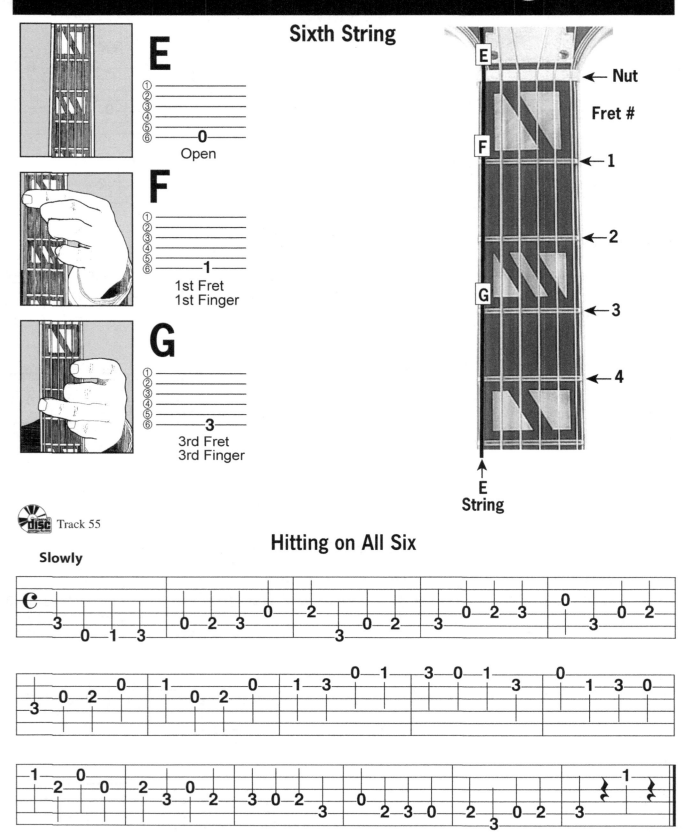

**Sixth String**

E — Open

F — 1st Fret, 1st Finger

G — 3rd Fret, 3rd Finger

Nut

Fret #

E String

Track 55

## Hitting on All Six

Slowly

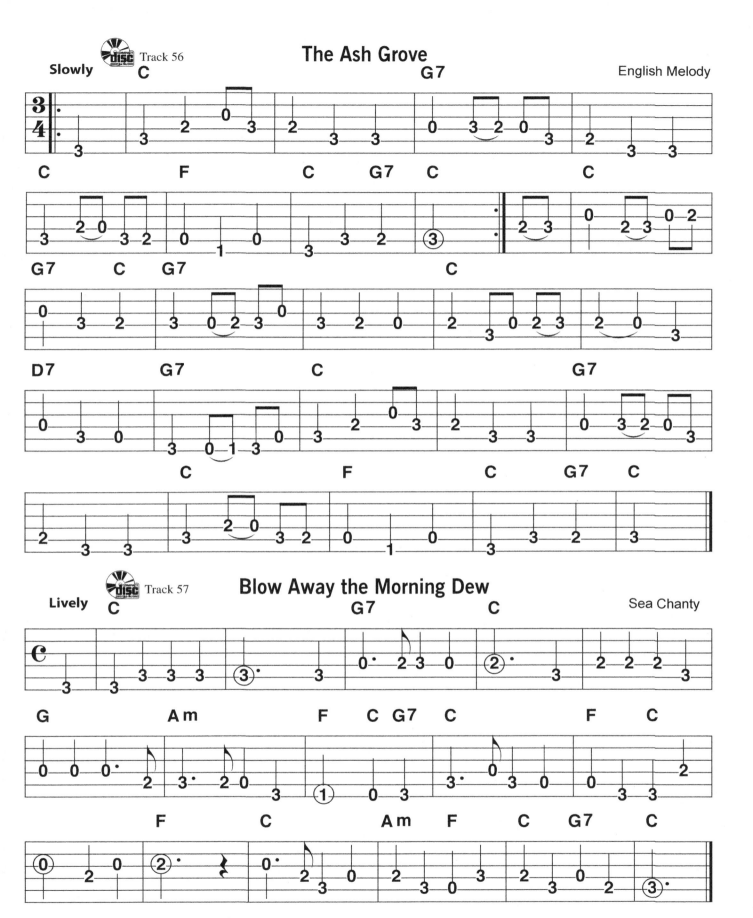

# Block Chords

When more than three notes are played together, the chord that results is called **block chord**. Block chords can contain four, five, or six notes. As with triads, play the notes quickly so they sound at the same time. Practice the following pieces which contain **triads** and **block chords**.

Track 58 **Black Is the Color of My True Love's Hair**

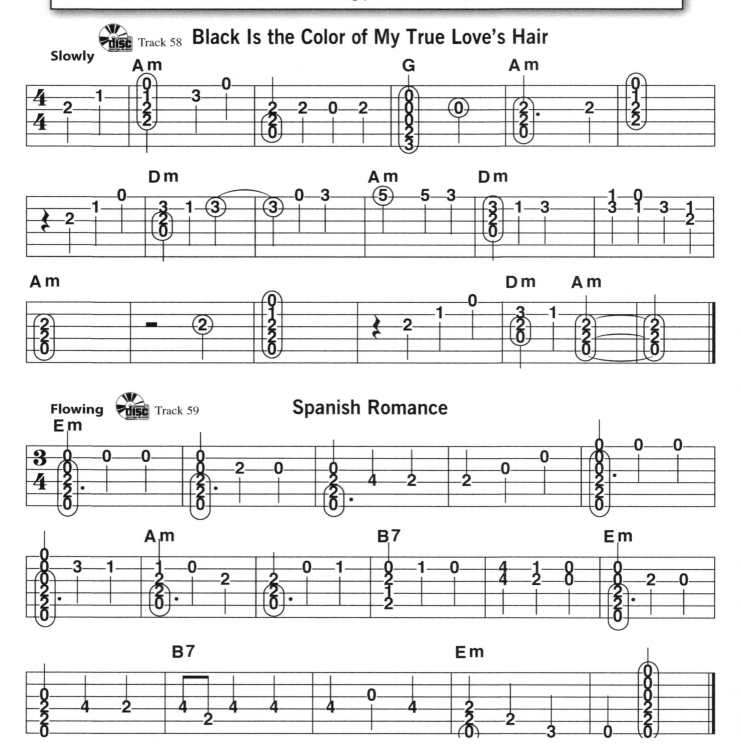

Track 59 **Spanish Romance**

# Chords in the Key of C Major

The key of C has three principal chords. They are C, F, and G7.

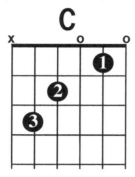 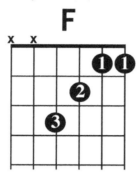 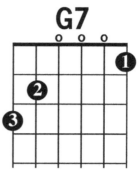

- The circles indicate the position where your fingers should be placed.
- Numerals inside circles indicate the fingers.
- "X" over the strings means that the strings are not to be played.
- "O" over the strings indicates the strings be played open.
- Place fingers in positions indicated by the circles and strike them all together.

## Chord Studies in C

 Track 60

╱ = Strum chord down across string      = Down – up strum

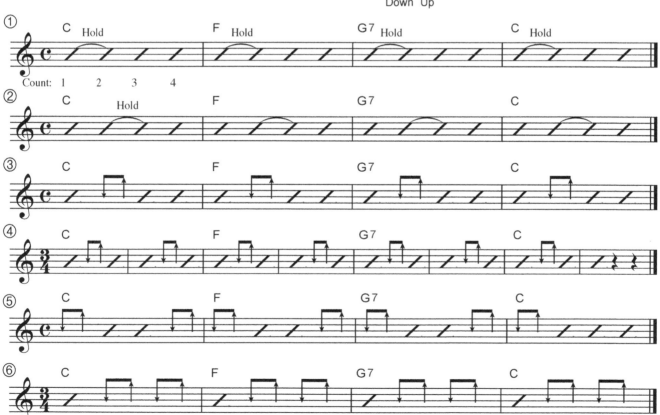

# The C Scale

## C Scale

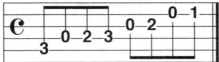

## Extended C Scale

## Velocity Study #1

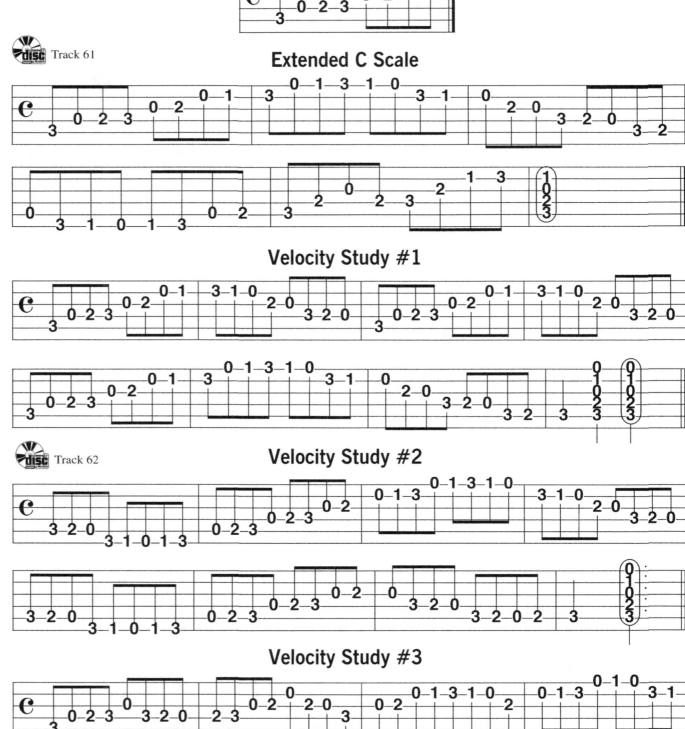

## Velocity Study #2

## Velocity Study #3

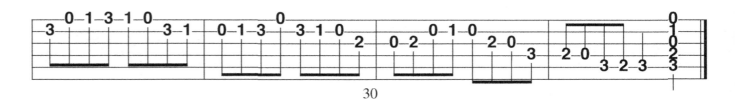

30

# Introducing the A Note

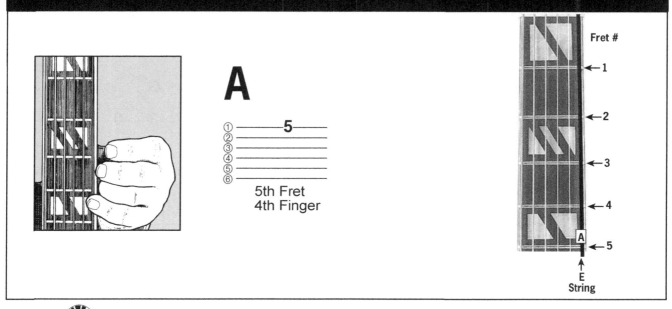

A

5th Fret
4th Finger

Fret #
← 1
← 2
← 3
← 4
A ← 5
↑ E String

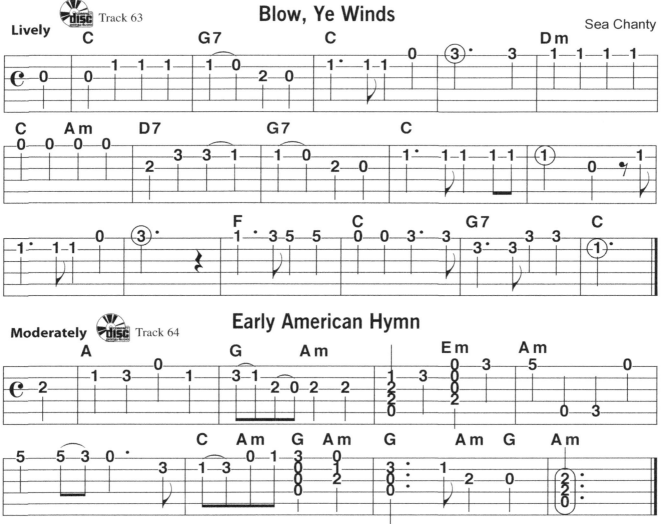

Blow, Ye Winds

Track 63

Lively

Sea Chanty

Early American Hymn

Moderately    Track 64

31

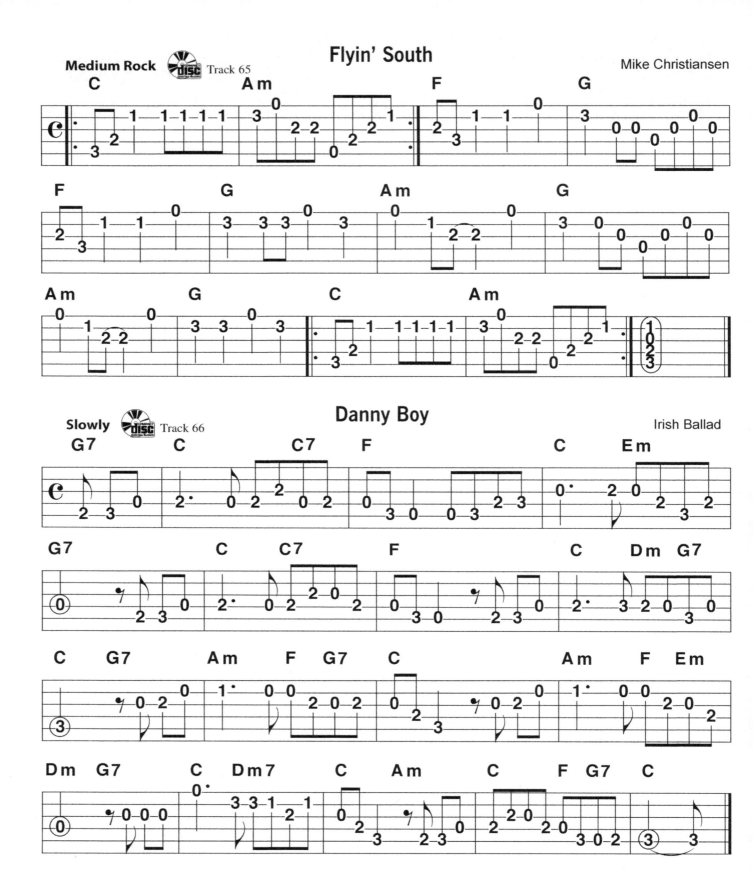

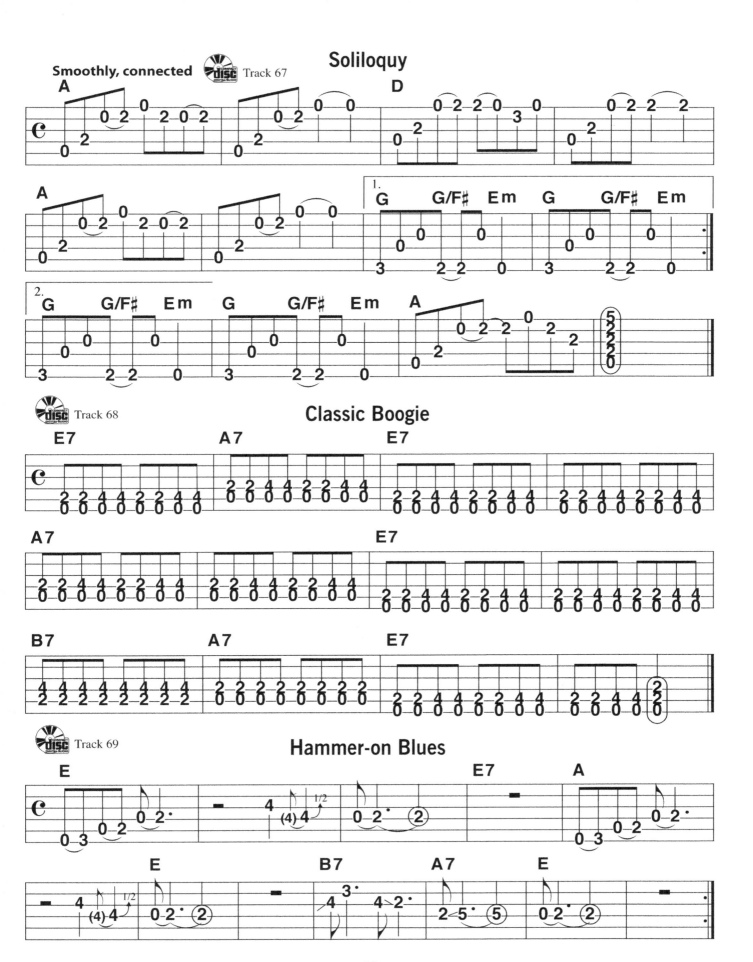

# Rock/Blues Solos Utilizing Lower Strings

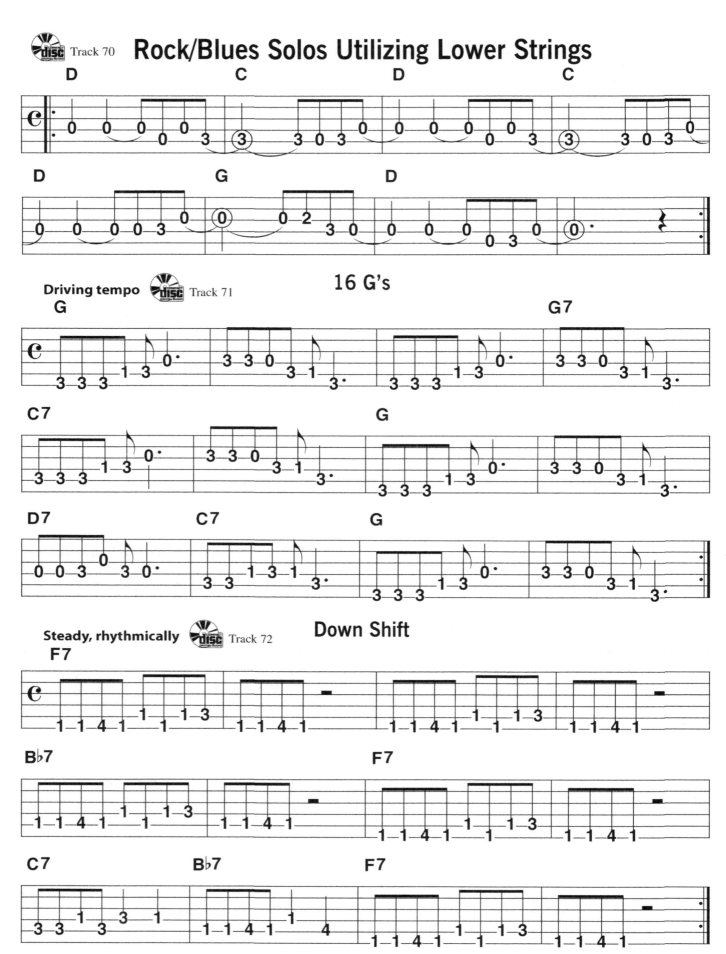

**Driving tempo** Track 71

## 16 G's

**Steady, rhythmically** Track 72 **Down Shift**

# The Key of A Minor

## The Chords in the Key of A Minor

m = minor

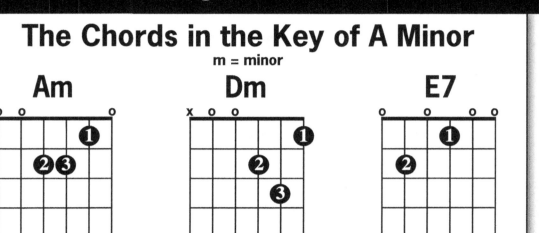

## Chord Studies in the Key of Am

Track 73

∕ = Strum chord down across strings

↓__↑ = Down – up strum
Down Up

# Key of A Minor

## A Natural Minor Scale

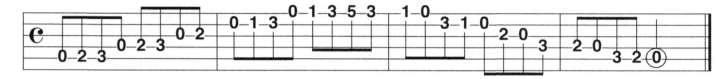

## Velocity Study

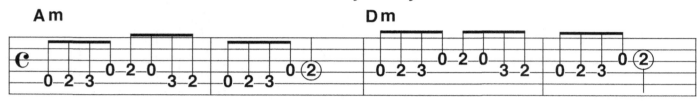

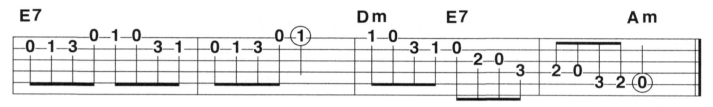

## A Harmonic Minor

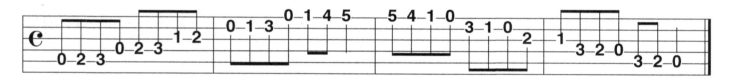

## Velocity Study

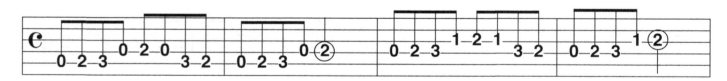

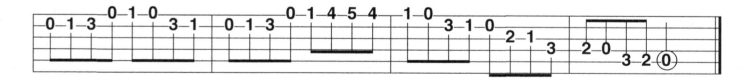

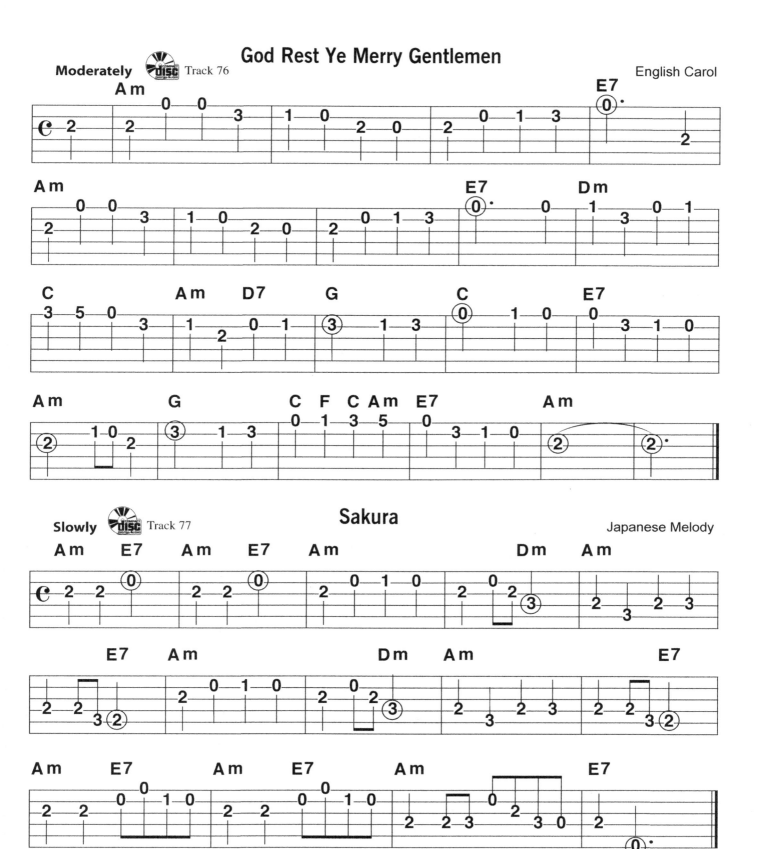

# D.C. al Fine

When this phrase appears at the end of a piece (**D.C. al Fine**) go back to the beginning and play until you see the word "**Fine**," which means "The End."

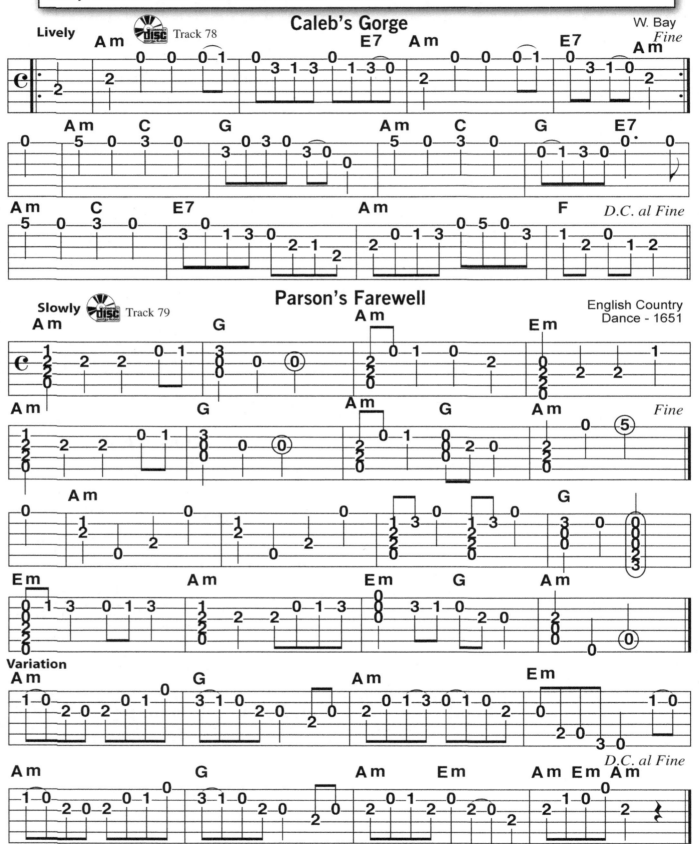

**Caleb's Gorge**

Lively — Track 78

W. Bay

**Parson's Farewell**

Slowly — Track 79

English Country
Dance - 1651

*D.C. al Fine*

# Eleven Mile Canyon

**Rousing tempo** 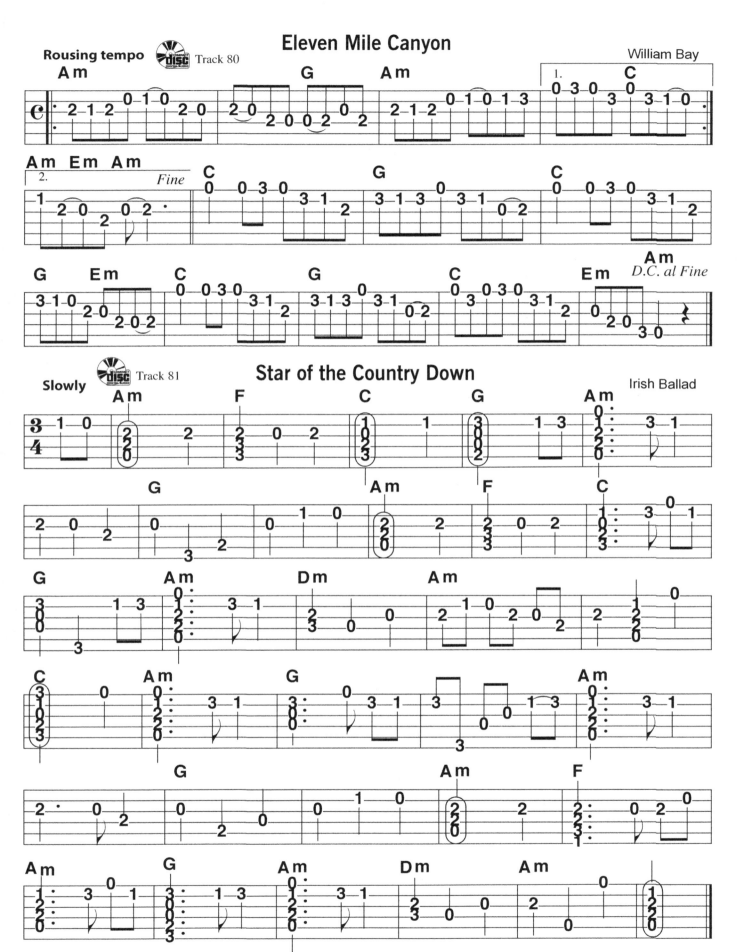 Track 80

William Bay

# Triplets

A **triplet** is a group of three notes played in the time of two notes of the same kind.

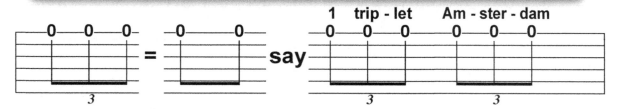

## Triplet Study

**Slowly** Track 82

William Bay

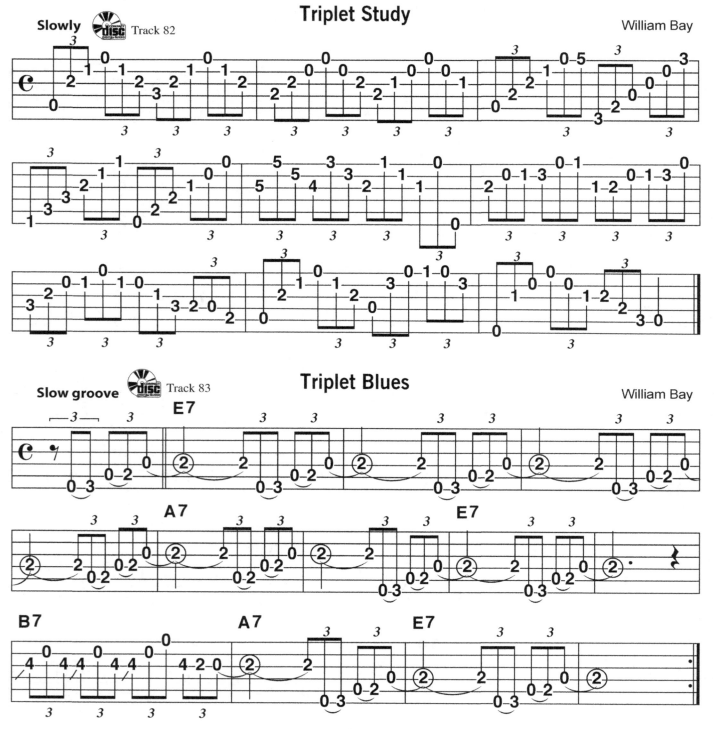

## Triplet Blues

**Slow groove** Track 83

William Bay

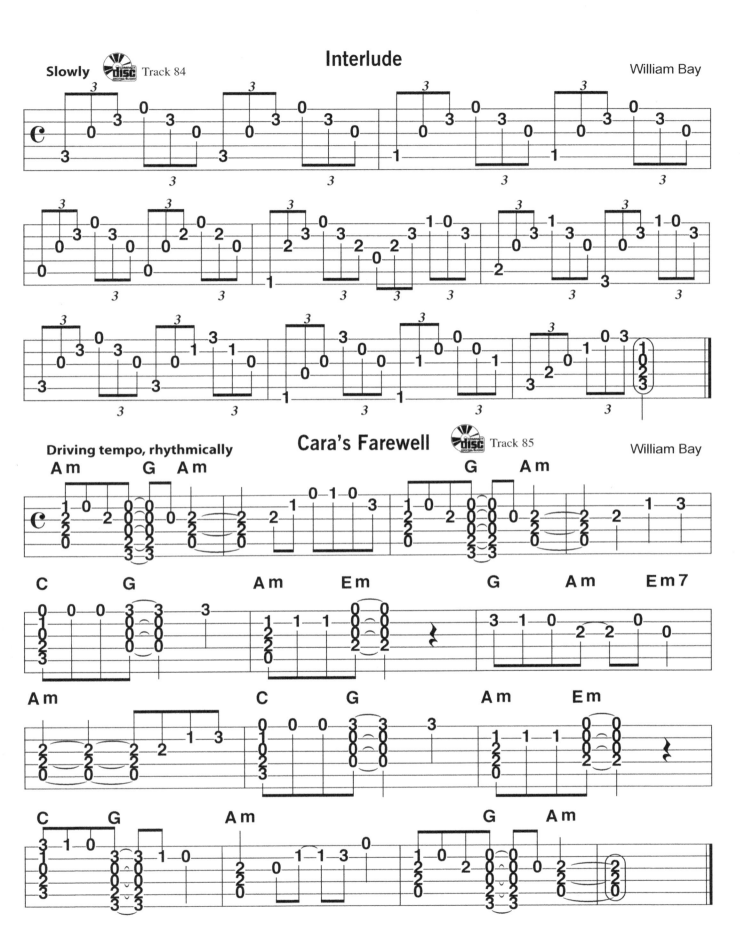

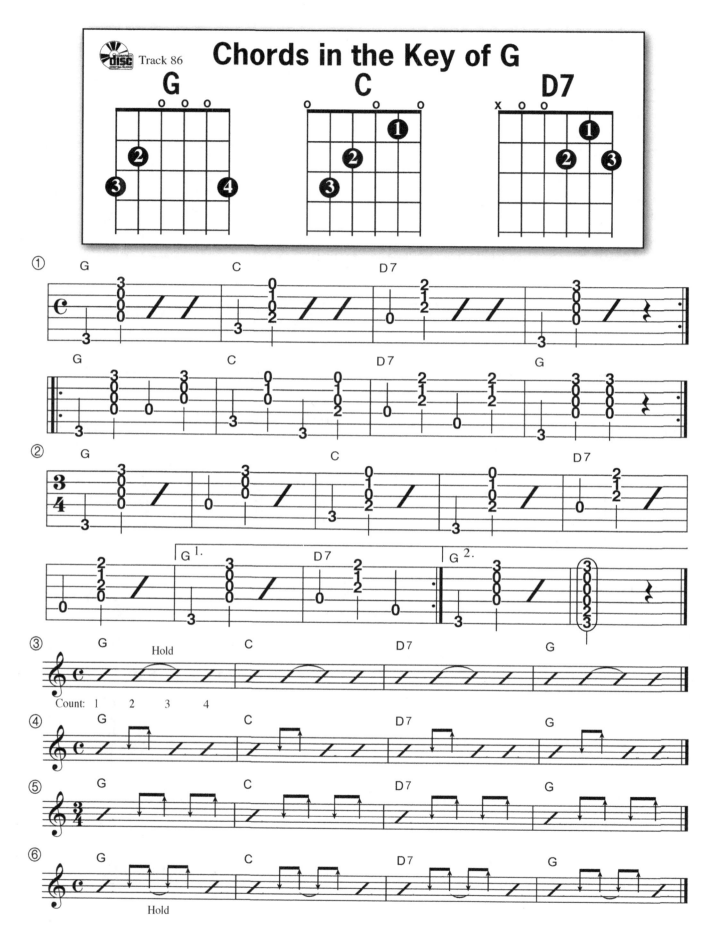

# G Solos
## Same As You

Mike Christiansen

Slowly, let notes ring  Track 87

## Far From Home

Shetland Island Reel

Medium tempo  Track 88

43

# Be Thou My Vision

Irish Hymn

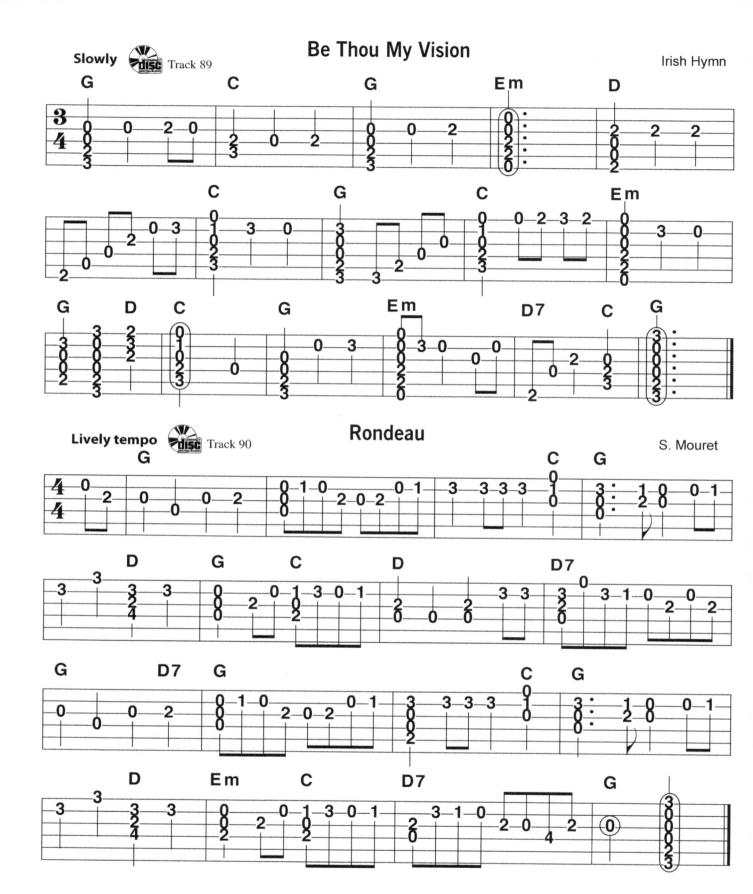

## Rondeau

S. Mouret

# Key of E Minor
## E Natural Minor Scale

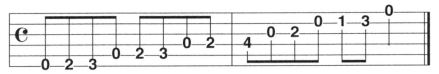

## Velocity Study #1

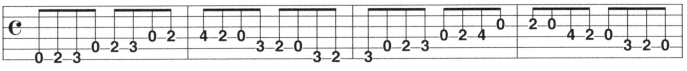

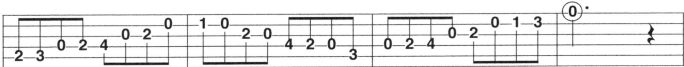

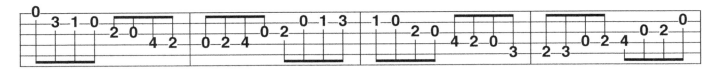

## E Harmonic Minor Scale

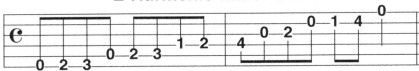

## Velocity Study #2

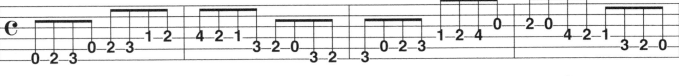

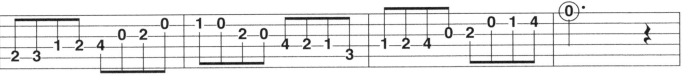

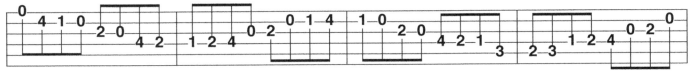

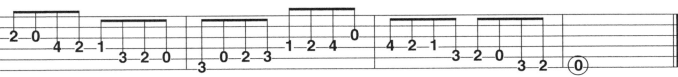

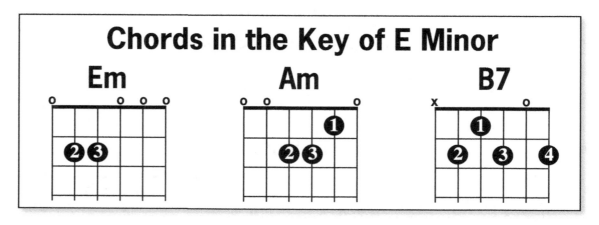

# Chords in the Key of E Minor

## Em  Am  B7

## Orchestration Styles

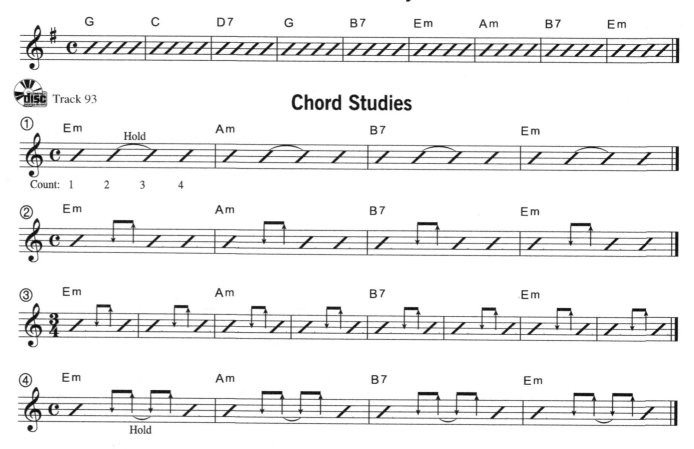

**Track 93**

## Chord Studies

# Shaker Dance

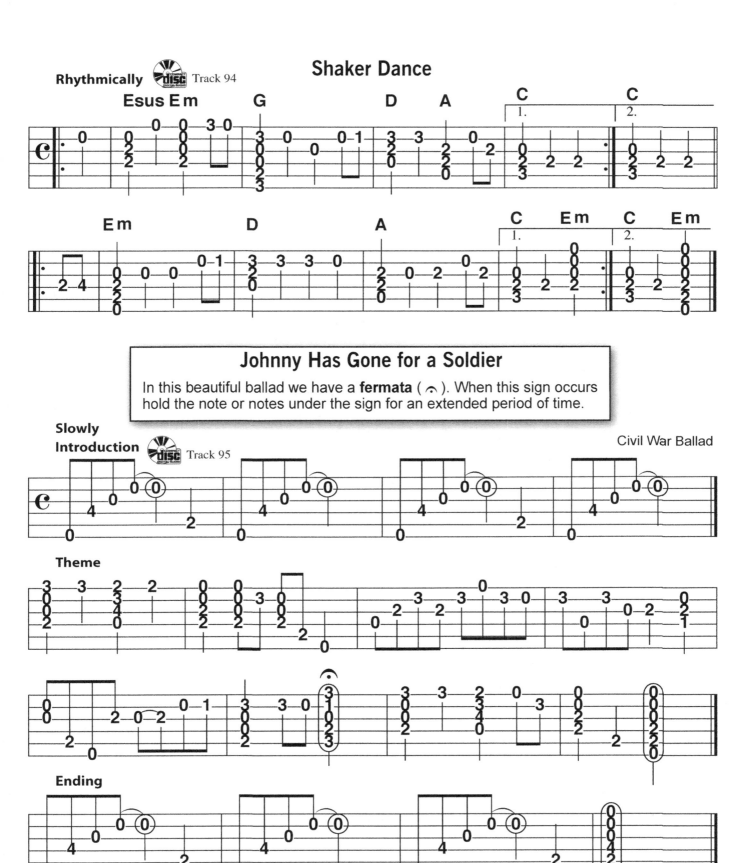

**Rhythmically** Track 94

## Johnny Has Gone for a Soldier

In this beautiful ballad we have a **fermata** ( ⌢ ). When this sign occurs hold the note or notes under the sign for an extended period of time.

**Slowly**
**Introduction** Track 95

Civil War Ballad

**Theme**

**Ending**

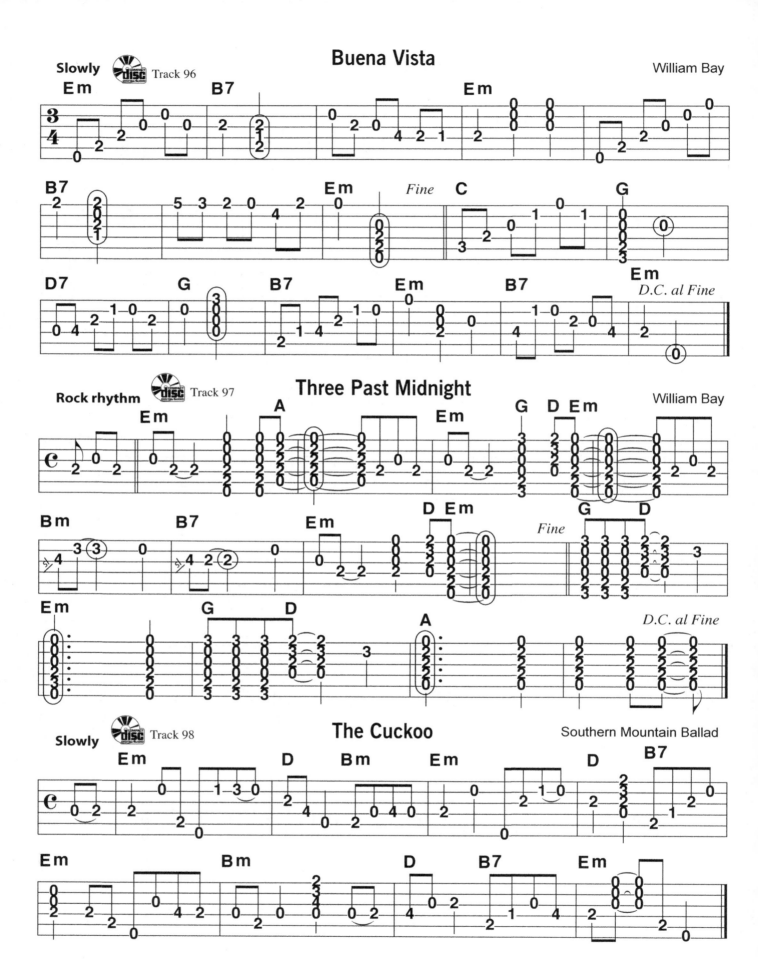

Made in the USA
Middletown, DE
05 October 2022